MONTESSORI BABY GUIDE

51 Simplified Tips to Nurture, Empower, and Have Fun with your Infant while Remaining True to the Montessori Tradition

Sanders
Certified Montessori Guide

Published by Iditatran Press (USA) 948 Hudson Street, New York, NY 10014, Iditatran Press (Australia) Iditatran Press 19489 Wollumburah St. Sydney NSW, Australia, (Canada) edition Iditatran, 2010, 39 Rue De Filbraet, Montreal, Quebec, Canada, M4P 24, (England) 39 Brighton, F2CR OLA

IDITATRAN PRESS

Foreword

During my years as both a Certified Montessori Teacher and a caregiver, I received numerous requests from parents for more information outlining practical methods to facilitate their children's development in a simplified, condensed manner that honored the Montessori way. The result is this book. I have restricted this material to simplified, comprehensive, and most importantly applicable lessons for parents, parents to be, and guardians. I Include fundamentals and ideas taken directly from my hours in the classroom, my time as a nanny, my personal studies, and from insights shared with others dedicated to the tradition. Happy Parenting!

Montessori Fundamentals

1. Providing both an environment and a structure in which a child can be independent, empowered, stimulated, and healthy.
2. Observing each child's movements, curiosities, likes, and dislikes on a daily basis, and appropriately modifying the structure or environment that surrounds them to encourage more growth, happiness, and independence.
3. Letting each child lead and then following their lead.
4. Recognizing that children naturally have *Absorbent Minds* and providing them with age appropriate toys and\or learning materials that nurture their innate way of learning.
5. Allowing children younger than three years of age to experience things directly, rather than teaching them abstract ideas.
6. Being minimally directive, especially regarding learning and playtime.
7. Always remembering that your child is a unique individual, and is not a lesser being.

0-6 months

1. Preparing the Sleeping Room

The purpose of the sleeping room is sleep. Because the newborn has just emerged from the womb, she is accustomed to an environment that is warm, quiet, and dark. It is important that the sleeping room has these fundamental characteristics. An ideal temperature is 68-72 degrees Fahrenheit. Experts disagree as to whether a room that is dead silent, or a room with white noise is preferable. You may wish to experiment with both. Once you find the one your baby prefers, stay consistent unless there is a sensible reason to vary. A Bassinet or Moses Basket is perfect for the first 4 months to simulate a womb-like environment. Choose a basket with low sides so the baby can still perceive most of her peripheral environment. At about four months, transition to a floor bed.

Benefit: A properly arranged Sleeping Room will provide a foundation for your baby, helping her feel safe, and providing her with positive boundaries.

2. The Floor Bed

While cribs may appear to serve the function of protecting your baby, they are in fact impeding your baby's range of movement and fostering a sense of dependence.

Choose a natural latex mattress such as an Ikea slat or tilt mattress. Fit a tight waterproof cover over the mattress, line with a sheet cover, and then, depending on room temperature, place a sheet and\or blanket atop baby for warmth. Place a large, soft rug beside the mattress. The rug should be at least as long and wide as the floor mat, space allowing. Obviously, care should be taken so that your baby does not have access to space heaters, electrical outlets, wires, or hard objects on which s\he could injure themselves should they roll off of their mat. It is important that the floor bed is started before six months, as it may be challenging to transition a baby that has already become accustomed to sleeping in a crib.

Benefit: A floor bed grants an infant freedom, a range of independence, self-esteem, and encourages decision-making. A crib restricts and impedes infants under the guise of protection. Babies are more likely to get injured in a crib than on a floor mat that has been situated in a well-arranged room.

3. Hang a Horizontal Mirror in your Infant's Sleeping Room

Affix a mirror to the wall in your infant's bedroom. The mirror should be approximately 4 feet long, but should be hung horizontally. The bottom should be approximately 3 inches from the floor so that your child can see her reflection. Make sure that the edges of the mirror are either framed or tapered so that she cannot cut herself on the glass when she becomes a toddler.

Benefit: A staple in the Montessori system, a mirror allows a child to watch her reflection and learn about her body's movements. Even before six months, baby can begin to conceptualize movements in relation to the reflection, which Maria Montessori believed boosted self-esteem. Mirrors also encourage infants to lift up their head during tummy time, thereby strengthening their neck, back, and core.

4. Movement Mat

A *Movement Mat* is a lightweight mat, mattress, or futon generally compromised of materials such as BPA-free foam. Movement Mat's should be soft, but not frumpy, clean, and compromised of materials that are pleasing to the touch. The mat should be a single, smooth plain and should not contain bumps, ridges, or valleys.

Movement Mat's are essential for your infant and should take the place of cribs and playpens, both of which impede baby's natural movements. The Movement Mat is not intended as a place for sleep, but as a place to move. If your baby should fall asleep, gently relocate her to the sleeping room. Because we are making an effort to give the baby structure, it is important to distinguish between areas of play, areas of sleep, dining areas, and eventually, toilet areas.

Benefit: Movement Mat's permit infants a sensation of independence, and foster autonomy and freedom of movement.

5. Suspend a Mobile above your Infant's Movement Mat

Although hanging a mobile is not unique to the Montessori System, the characteristics of the Mobile and how it is hung are more specified than common parenting schools of thought. First, most Montessori experts agree that the mobile should not be hung above the place of sleep, but should be hung above the movement mat. For the first 3-4 months the mobile should feature combinations of black and white, and should be suspended approximately 10-12 inches above your baby's heart. Never hang a mobile directly above your baby's head, as this could lead to eyestrain. Simple and natural materials such as wood are always preferred over plastic. After approximately four months, you may wish to add mobiles with colors. During baby's first year, four mobiles should be acquired, and circulated out every 3 weeks; this keeps baby's attention engaged.

Benefits: Mobiles help develop visual sense, strengthen eye muscles, and encourage coordination. Most Montessori practitioners recommend avoiding plastic mobiles.

6. Hang Framed Art Prints in Sleeping Room

Maria Montessori believed that parents should create an environment filled with beauty. In the sleeping room this can be nurtured by hanging 1-2 prints on each wall. Art should be both pleasing to the eye, and colorful. Most infants respond best to combinations of reds, yellows, oranges, blues, and greens. Impressionists such as Van Gogh, Monet, Manet, Renoir, Cezanne, and Degas are favorites. One to two paintings per wall are sufficient, but more than that is not recommended as too many may prove over-stimulating. Paintings should not be cartoony, or feature animals personified as people (i.e. wearing clothes or driving automobiles) Instead, selections should be mature, and invite introspection. Although totally subjective, I recommend landscapes over portraits. Some experts recommend keeping loud colors such as reds and oranges to a minimum in places of sleep. Use best judgment.

Benefit: Many infants begin to explore visually before they begin to crawl. Therefore, combinations of contrasting colors can help baby's brain develop while providing both stimulation and relaxation.

7. Pacifiers Versus Teether Balls

In their first six months, your infant will begin to start using their tongue and lips to form sounds. It is crucial that they learn as quickly as possible, that by vocalizing (not crying) they can get your attention. This early discovery allows them the epiphany that their voices and their words (or babbles) are incredibly powerful tools. The age-old pacifier, which may seem like a harmless staple of parenthood, actually interrupts this natural process, and encourages infants to scream for attention. Because the pacifier represents a nipple, the child suckles more out of natural order, than as a conscious, deliberate act. However, because no milk is obtained from the pacifier, the child is left to simply suckle for the sake of suckling. This suckling may quiet the child, but there are some Psychologists who theorize that the pacifier may actually encourage oral fixation and addictive behavior later in life. Because infants love to suck and explore with their mouths, a *Teether Ball* is preferred.

Benefit: Teether Balls unique shapes prevent them from remaining idle in the mouth. Many Teether Balls can be grasped by infants while suckling, potentially providing a head start on motor coordination.

8. Breastfeeding

Breast-feeding is a time of bonding for both mother and child. Although not always feasible, it is recommended that mother devote her attention to her nursing infant. This could include stroking baby's head, caressing his arms or leg, and not allowing her bond to become distracted by outside stimuli such as television, phone calls, texting, internet, or even books. Whenever possible, light classical music can be a wonderful addition to the breastfeeding experience. As a mother, you may notice that baby often stares intently up at your face. When your baby does this, whisper his name, or tell him a story. This will help him associate your voice. Remember: Your baby is like a sponge absorbing all the stimuli in his environment.

Benefit: Abstaining from outside distractions while breastfeeding deepens the bond between mother and baby.

9. Thanking your Baby

As a parent you make many sacrifices, so it may seem counterintuitive to say *thank you* to the little person to whom you are waiting on hand and food. However, saying thank you to your baby has many benefits. First, it habituates parents to positive interaction. Thank You's soothe both parent and child. In addition, experts recommend talking to your baby to facilitate motor development, socialize, and increase cognitive function. If you can sincerely thank your baby after most specific (but not all) interactions, you will develop a stronger bond and a stronger resilience to the inevitable challenges that being a parent entails.

Benefit: People who say thank you more often are proven to have stronger willpower and lower blood pressure. Because your children model you, saying sincere Thank You's will set a wonderful example.

10. Picking baby up (General overview)

Except when your baby is asleep, always ask permission to pick her up. After the assumed confirmation offer a gentle, but sincere *thank you*, even if you are responding to your babies cries. This rule is especially important for fathers. Because infants are more prone to attach to mothers early on -due to mother's scent and the reward of breast milk, it is beneficial for baby to associate a specific phrase spoken in a specific tone to anchor a feeling of safety. Remember: Routine provides the positive foundation for security.

For example: Good Morning Lucy, may I please pick you up? To end: Thank you Lucy, I'm going to set you back down now, I love you.

Benefit: A parent who consistently handles their baby in a comforting manner, and always begins and ends each interaction with a similar toned request or statement will inspire more comfort, confidence, and trust.

11. Yes Environment Instead of a No Environment

During their maturity, babies have a tendency to find just about everything in their environment appealing. Arrange your living room, kitchen, bathroom, hallways, and bedrooms in both an *accommodating* and *aesthetically pleasing* manner. Start with a single room. Could a crawling baby explore without your interruption? If not, consider making some simple changes. For instance: If there are bookshelves that baby could reach up and pull books off of, consider relocating the books to higher shelves and\or storage. If there is a priceless heirloom on the coffee table, why not relocate it to the mantle? Arrange each room so that there is no need to redirect.

Benefit: A *Yes Environment* will ward off problems before they start, and will ease the mind of the parents when baby is exploring her new world. Positive reinforcement is always favored to discipline.

12. Music

Play music for your baby at set times, keep volume low and bear in mind that babies developing ears are more sensitive to sound than adults. When experiencing music, many newborns may not seem to respond for the first few months, but have patience. W.A. Mozart and J.S. Bach are the most studied composers, and their works seem to have consistent positive results. Others composers who have gained acclaim are F. Chopin, L.V. Beethoven, and J. Brahms. For best results, compile a list -one track at a time, for one week. Introducing a single piece (as opposed to an entire album or an endless stream) will allow your baby to make associations faster than simply playing a wide spectrum of pieces every day.

Benefit: Exposure to certain classical music improves spatial reasoning, helps form neural pathways, calms baby, and stimulates the immune system. As a pianist, baby lover, and classical music fanatic, I have included my recommended playlist. Feel free to deviate from it according to your own taste.

Week 1 The Aquarium by Camille St. Saens
Week 2 (add) Piano Concerto No. 21 by W.A. Mozart
Week 3 (add to list) Jesu Man's Desiring by J.S. Bach
Week 4 (add to list) Blue Danube by J. Strauss
Week 5 (new list) Cello Suite No. 1 (Prelude) by J.S. Bach
Week 6 (add to list) Fur Elise by L.V. Beethoven
Week 7 (add to List) Waltz No. 2 by D. Shostakovich
Week 8 (add to list) Op. 9, No. 2 in E flat major, Andante, by F. Chopin
Week 1 Reset and begin new list.

13. Clothing

A newborn's skin is extremely sensitive. For this reason, clothes that directly touch baby's skin should be made of natural fibers such as cotton or bamboo. White and pastels are preferred over bright colors, as they do not contain dyes. Outer layers should fit snugly, but should not restrict circulation. Obviously, the weather will dictate many of your choices. Clothes that do not directly touch the skin should be comfortable first, and colorful second. After eight months I advocate elastic pants, which can be pulled on and off easily, white cotton t-shirts, and Velcro tennis shoes.

Benefit: First, clothing that can be pulled on and off easily will ensure that circulation is not restricted. Second, as your baby develops, clothes that can be pulled on and taken off quickly will encourage her to get dressed on her own. In your daily schedule, any opportunity to limit your baby's dependence on you will reduce stress and increase both productivity and happiness.

14. Turn Off and Cover: Television, Computer, & Tablet Screens

The American Academy of Pediatrics has performed extensive studies on the subject of television and electronic media. Their findings state that media "Has potentially negative effects and no known positive effects upon children younger than 2 years."

Computer and Television Screens are composed of millions of pixels. When video is streamed, babies developing eyes are naturally drawn toward the flashing pixels. Over time, screens may inhibit learning, weaken eye muscles, and stunt certain areas of development.

Although not specifically addressed by Maria Montessori, it is my conclusion that screens should be turned off; and ideally put away or covered entirely.

Benefit: limiting exposure to screens will ensure that your baby's brain develops naturally.

15. Lighting and Curtains

Natural lighting is preferred over artificial lighting. In cases where natural lighting is not available, soft lighting is optimal. Light in the sleeping room may be dimmed when the sun goes down to assist with baby's natural Circadian rhythms. If you live in an area where streetlights invade the sleeping room, you may wish to use 2 curtains. On the outer side use a darker toned curtain (black out curtain) to block out the light. On the inside a curtain with a simple, organic pastel color is optimal. Eggshell blue may be the best color to help induce a sense of calm.

Benefit: Blackout curtains will allow your baby to sleep more naturally, while organic pastels will soften the room.

16. Communication

Except for when your baby is sleeping, waking, nursing, or upset, you should speak to him in a clear, direct, and warm voice. Resist the urge to talk at your baby, instead, communicate with him. Ask him questions and observe his responses. You may be surprised by the non-verbal answers you'll get to the questions you ask with sincerity. Practice repeating phrases 7-10 times per day; use the same sentences and the same tone of voice. Obvious choices might be. "Hello my sweet (babies name) I am (your name) and I love you very much." Another exercise would be to practice using the same phrase at specific times of the day: "Good morning (babies name) did you enjoy your breakfast this morning?"

Benefit: Speaking to your baby in a similar manner (for the first few months) will help their cognition and speech recognition.

17. Advice for Father's To Be:

During the first few weeks it is natural for baby to form a stronger bond with mother than father. However, there are a few tricks father's and fathers-to-be can implement to strengthen their bond with their new son or daughter. Your first task is to be consistent. Remember that during the first 2-4 weeks your infant becomes associated with smells and taste first, touch second, sounds third, and sight last. Because smell has such a strong association for babies, take inventory of your toiletries. Are any of them harsh or chemical? You will want to avoid aftershaves and colognes as they mask your natural smell and are too harsh for baby's delicate senses. In terms of shaving creams, moisturizer, body wash, shampoos, conditioners, and laundry detergents, find a single brand that you know you can commit to for at least the next six months and remain consistent. Abruptly changing toiletries or soaps during the first six months could confuse your newborn, and when you pick her up in the night to soothe her back to sleep, you may find you have a harder time calming her down.

Benefit: Be consistent with toiletries allows your baby to attach to you more naturally.

18. Stroking Babies Arm (The Right Way)

Stroking your baby increases immunity, boosts good feeling neurotransmitters, and is soothing. There is a simple hack unknown to many parents. *Stroking can be used to calm or to stimulate your baby, but it all depends on the direction in which you stroke.* Babies get upset for different reasons, so if it is bedtime and you wish to soothe your baby with stroking, stroke the arm *away* from your babies heart (Ex: stroke from babies elbow, toward babies wrist, lift your hand up, and repeat) Try it on yourself now, and you will see that this has a soothing effect. Want to stimulate your baby? Gently stroke along her arm *toward* her heart (ex: Start at the wrist, and gently drag your fingers toward babies elbow. When you reach the elbow, stop, lift your hand, bring back to wrist and repeat) Stroking in both directions (i.e. back and forth) is not recommended. In the majority of instances you will want to use the calming stroke (away from the heart)

Benefit: Learning the proper touch technique will aide you in your interactions with your baby.

19. Your House is a Museum

At about 3 months, make it a weekly practice to take your baby on a tour of your house. Act as if you were a museum guide giving a tour, pausing at places of interest. Allow your baby a moment to take in what is before them. Then, briefly explain what you are showing them. Dedicate extra time to areas that baby displays interest in. If there is something that you are fond of, share it with your baby. Do you have a sculpture or a stained glass window in your house? How about a fountain in your yard? If not, don't fret; your newborn will be equally enthralled by the sink in your kitchen and the pine tree in your front yard.

Benefit: This practice facilitates the sensory stimulation that is so important to baby's growth and development.

20. Children's Books (for baby's)

Because infants are just beginning to conceptualize the difference between fantasy and reality, Maria Montessori advocated for non-fiction books. The logic being that fantasy books could delay comprehension. If you despair over the thought of (temporarily) shelving timeless children's classics I've got great news for you, you can start introducing them after the child's third birthday. Until then, choose books with lots of photographs of mammals, birds, or fish. Seashell and flower identification guides are both wonderfully fun, especially when they contain large pictures. If you must include a fairytale, forgo books that personify animals or inanimate objects (such as trains) as people.

Benefit: Choosing the right books will help ensure your baby matures in a natural and healthy manner.

21. Take Baby Outside

So long as your baby is healthy, start taking them outside at about three weeks.

The sounds, smells, and sights are all wonderful stimuli for the young mind, and the fresh air will be great for you as a parent. Gardens and Parks are both ideal, but front and back yards can prove just as stimulating. Let your baby feel the sensation of grass or sand on their bare feet. Talk to them about the things you see around you. If there isn't a flower available to pick, then a leaf will prove just as fascinating. Always be mindful of weather conditions, and dress baby appropriately. Base your exposure time on weather.

Benefit: Brief periods of exposure to fresh air will boost your baby's immunity and will aide in development. When one parents takes a baby outside, it can provide the other parent with some much-needed alone time.

22. Choosing the right Child Safety Seat for your Baby

The importance of investing in the right child safety seat cannot be overstated.

The Government has many resources available at websites such as www.safercar.gov Start by doing research on individual brands. Once you have selected one, make sure that it matches your baby's height and weight requirements. Most experts recommend rear-facing seats for newborns and infants, however, base your decision on the type of vehicle you drive, the size of your baby, and the recommendations of the safety seat manufacturer. If you have questions contact the manufacturer and/or refer to reputable resources. It is critical for new parents to understand that using a safety seat improperly can be just as bad (if not worse) than not using one at all.

Benefit: Properly used car seats save lives.

23. Introducing Your Baby to the Child Safety Seat

Rather than simply bringing your child out to the car and fitting them into their car seat, make certain that their first experience is a positive one by doing a practice run indoors. Begin by choosing a day at least two days in advance of the day you plan to go driving with your baby. Place the car seat on top of your babies mat. Allow them to discover it without trying to 'do anything' with the seat. Most babies will naturally take an interest in this new addition to their environment. Due to the straps on the seat, do not leave your baby alone with the car seat, as there is a slim chance they could climb in and potentially endanger themselves. Instead, observe them quietly. After about ten minutes, gently pick up your baby. If baby is quiet and relaxed, gently set her in the seat. Speak calmly to her in the manner that you usually do. If baby is calm, let her remain in the seat. Sit beside the seat and touch her gently. After about five minutes, gently strap baby in. Making sure that she is comfortable. Observe. After approximately five minutes, remove baby from seat. Ideally you will want to replicate this exercise at least two times before going to the car.

Benefit: This exercise allows babies to get associated with car seats in stages. It also allows you the optimum opportunity for control of the situation.

Leaving it until the day of your first outing could prove extremely stressful. This exercise will also allow you to observe your baby in the seat, something you won't be able to do with as much dedication when you are focused on driving.

6-12 Months

24. Practice Getting Down On Your Baby's Level

At approximately 5-9 months, sight becomes the most dominant of the 5 senses. At about this period of development, your baby's eyes become their primary filter for understanding their environment. In the first few months of development, the practice of lowering yourself might not seem especially significant. However, as you begin to start communicating with your baby, it is important that your baby feels like your equal. When you tower over another person and 'speak down to them' it presents many challenges. First, it makes it harder for your baby to hear you speaking. Second, it makes it harder for your baby to see the non-verbal cues expressed on your face. Whether you're kneeling or lying, getting on your baby's level will make playtime fun now, and communication easier later.

Benefit: Spending time on babies level strengthens your bond and helps baby to communicate. When your baby sees your lips moving he will be moved to try speaking. When he sees you smiling he will be comforted.

25. Construct Low Shelves

A single set of low shelves in the infant's bedroom provides many benefits. First, they give your infant something to crawl toward in their early months. In later months, low shelves prepare them to be more autonomous in their decision-making. When building shelves, it is important to get down low and try to see from your baby's perspective. Shelves should be simple, and constructed of wood or durable materials. Shelves holding books should be linear, and singular in paint tone (i.e. all white or all blue). Having intricate patterns, or detailed scenes on shelves is generally discouraged, as it may conflict with the linear and orderly appearance of the books.

Benefit: Low shelves allow infants to conceptualize and familiarize themselves with order and neatness. Low shelves empower infants and teach them to be responsible with their belongings.

26. Sitting Place

The use of high chairs is highly discouraged in the Montessori Tradition, as it prevents infants and toddlers from placing their feet on the floor. When a child's feet touch the floor, (or an artificial ledge constructed into the chair) they feel grounded. In the early years, this benefit may seem negligible, but as they mature, infants will begin to feel powerless and totally reliant upon their parents to free them. Mealtime may no longer represent a time of enjoying food, but a period of imprisonment or punishment. Powerless children are more likely to rebel and resist food, while children who feel grounded are more likely do develop positive eating habits.

Benefit: When toddlers outgrow their high chair, chaos often ensues; as the toddler uses the newfound freedom to play and 'act out' rather then eat. If a high chair is never used, weaning them off the high chair does not present this problem.

27. Choose breakable Plates and Glassware

One of the most important aspects of the Montessori System is the promotion of breakable glassware and\or ceramic plates over Sippy Cups and plastic\disposable plates. I recommend creating a 'set' containing:

1 small glass
1 small ceramic bowl
1 small ceramic plate
1 small spoon
1 small fork
1 small butter knife

The plate should be of the same color and material as yours. Monitor your child as you introduce these items. This subject is covered in more detail in the second book in our series, the Montessori Baby 12-36 months.

Benefit: In addition to being more aesthetically pleasing, breakable plates and glassware promote a sense of responsibility, as baby learns that there are natural consequences that occur from respecting objects of value.

28. Toys

Toys should be pleasing to the touch. Wood is generally preferred over plastic and Rubber wood is especially favored because of its durability. Rubber wood is also environmentally friendly and is not prone to chipping or wood burrs.

Although some brands advertise being Montessori friendly, it is important to verify that the toy meets recommended Montessori (and your) standards. When selecting (or constructing) a toy, simple design is preferred.

As infants develop they begin to respond to shapes, colors, and sounds, so make sure that you take these three factors into account. Are the shapes, colors and sounds that the toy makes pleasing?

Your baby is an individual, and as such, he or she will respond more favorably to some toys than others. Do not be disheartened if your baby does not take interest in a toy initially. Just be patient with them, you may be surprised that a toy shunned one week is soon baby's favorite.

29. Rattles

Rattles are one of the oldest and most culturally ubiquitous toys of earth. Many cultures discovered that rattles are a wonderful way to stimulate a baby's relationship to sound.

Benefits: Rattles are a great way to demonstrate cause and effect. With a few shakes, baby begins to internalize: *When I shake this object it makes a rattling sound.* This empowers baby with a notion that they can affect their environment.

What to look for: The rattle should be constructed of wood, with a handle grip that is not too large for your infants hand. Assure that the rattle works by shaking it before you purchase it. The rattling sound should be easy to replicate. Bear in mind that if it is hard for you to create a sound, it will be much harder for your infant.

30. Crocheted Soft Balls Crocheted Soft Balls are small, plum sized balls that are interweaved together, often in a circle. The texture of crocheted soft balls provides a delightful sensation on little fingers.
Benefits: Soft balls introduce a new texture to baby's world. Textures are fundamental to keeping holding baby's attention. Squeezing the soft balls strengthens their grip.
What to look for: Crocheted Softballs can be made at home or purchased on sites like Etsy. Softballs should be durable enough that they don't unravel.

31. Natural Wooden Blocks

Wooden blocks are popular in many cultures, as they are inexpensive and can be arranged to form simple patterns or structures.

Benefits: Blocks allow baby to practice grasping with their fingers and hands. They also provide the empowering freedom to construct and break down simple structures. When blocks of different sizes are used, it allows baby to conceptualize differentiate architectural sizes. Cleaning up blocks builds discipline.

What to look for: Blocks should be large enough to prevent choking, but small enough for you baby to manage. Blocks should be lightweight and easy to maneuver. Refrain from simply having a box in which blocks are thrown, instead use a piece of wood (like a puzzle) where blocks are put into place according to size or shape. This doubles the learning and the fun!

32. Wooden Shape Puzzles

Wooden Shape Puzzles are like oversized, simplified jigsaw puzzles. They should be constructed with easy handles for infant to grip and contain pieces of varying shapes (i.e. square, circle, triangle) that coordinate with pegs of varying primary colors. An ideal infant puzzle should have between 3 and 6 pieces.

Benefits: Wooden Shape Puzzles encourage spatial awareness and help develop fine motor skills. Being able to arrange puzzles repetitiously helps build confidence.

What to look for: Puzzles should be color-coded. Pieces should be large enough to prevent choking.

33. Permanence Box:
A Permanence Box is a wooden box featuring a horizontal wooden plank across the top or side. A round hole or series of holes in the plank allows a ball to disappear and then reappear.

Benefits: Permanence Boxes strengthen the recognition of cause and effect, lengthen concentration, and help baby development a sense of *Object Permanence,* the idea that something exists even when it is out of sight.

What to look for: Ball should be large enough to prevent choking, but small enough to fit in babies grip. Although any color is acceptable, red and orange are optimal as they are both easier for baby to see, and easier for parents to locate should the ball make its way onto the floor.

34. Wooden Stackers: Wooden Stackers are 3 dimensional structures that can be constructed, and de-constructed by stacking the parts on a hard surface. Like all toys, you will want to demonstrate to your baby how the stackers work. Once you have assembled and dissembled your structure, allow your infant time to play with the pieces. Do not be discouraged if she begins by placing the pieces in her mouth! This is a natural part of learning. In no time at all she will likely be constructing a stack.

Benefits: Stackers familiarize baby with the concepts of small, smaller, smallest, and large, larger, largest. They also nurture baby's spatial awareness. Stackers empower baby with the notion that they have creative control over an external part of their world. The earlier a baby can discover this, the earlier they can begin to develop.

What to look for: Wood should be durable and not prone to chipping. Color-coded wood is preferable to non-painted wood.

35. Nesting Toys

Nesting toys feature smaller pieces or dolls that fit into increasingly larger pieces or dolls. A famous example would be Russian Dolls. Maria Montessori recommended simple, eye pleasing shapes, such as circles or globes.

Benefit: In addition to spatial awareness and visual perception. Nesting toys empower cognitive reasoning. "If I can assemble and disassemble these toys, I wonder what else I can do?"

What to look for: Pieces should fit together and separate easily. Make the sure the smallest piece is not so delicate that it could be broken easily, and that the largest piece is not so large that baby can't handle it.

36. Shape Sorter

Shapes Sorters come in many, many different styles. We advocate natural materials, such as wood over plastic. Going on a *less is more* principal, select a Shape Sorter with a limited amount of pieces. As your baby matures, advance to Shape Sorters with more challenging designs.

Benefits: When baby succeeds in placing parts together it helps them gain confidence. Shape Sorters also help baby develop motor skills, shape and size recognition, and hand eye coordination.

What to look for: Choose a reputable company which constructs Shape Sorters out of wood.

37. Spinning Tops

Spinning Tops are a wonderful choice for a toy. When you first introduce the top to your baby's environment, show your baby how to spin it. After a few spins, allow them to grasp it in their hands. Then you may ask for the top back, and if they hand it to you, spin it again, or you may wait until they set it down of their own accord. When they set it down, spin it again.

Benefits: Spinning tops are simple, safe, inexpensive, durable, and time-tested.

What to look for: Tops should be wooden, and made by a reputable maker. Be especially careful of splinters. Take care that tops are not so small that could be swallowed.

38. Imbucare Box

An Imbucare Box is a hollow wooden cubical box with a shape specific hole cut into the top. Common shapes include triangles, squares, diamonds, ovals, rectangles, and circles. A corresponding wooden shape can then be deposited into the box and, if baby wishes, retrieved from a window or door.

Benefits: Imbucare Boxes strengthen the concept of object permanence, boost self-esteem, and help baby develop problem-solving abilities.

What to Look for: Both the box and the accompanying pieces should be wooden. If using boxes with slots for different shapes, it is important that shapes are represented by different colors.

39. Activity: Pouring Objects

Although often not seen as toys, pouring can be a supreme pleasure for infants. Begin by allowing your infant to pour solid objects such as buttons, nuts, or uncooked beans between two bowls. Once finished, allow him to dive his hands into the bowls and squish the contents. Then when you feel he is ready, graduate to pouring water.

Benefits: Pouring lengthens attention span, facilitates cause and effect, promotes cognitive skills, improves depth perception, and familiarizes infants with the concept of ratios.

What to Look for: Solid glass bowls with a wide mouth, 1 pitcher, and buttons, beads, nuts, or water to pour.

40. Carrying Time

During the first few months of development, it is important to hold your infant so that she can bond with you. However, at approximately the six-month mark it is crucial that you allow your infant ample time to explore her space. Holding her may upset or irritate her. It may be challenging to find the right balance, but use your instincts and go off of the clues that she gives you. Like adults, many baby's moods correspond with specific times of the day. You may notice that picking up your baby in the morning is generally wonderful, but in the afternoon she fidgets or cries. Working off this knowledge you may wish to hold your baby in the morning, and let her crawl in the afternoon, or vice versa.

Benefit: Limiting carrying time allows babies to develop a sense of independence and to explore their surroundings, both of which are critical for development.

41. Activity: Smooth, Rough, And Crinkly

One of the keys of the Montessori method is hands on learning. The practice is to let your baby touch and feel things, then to follow by allowing them (and occasionally helping them) make the correlating connection. An effective game for babies of approximately 11+ months is called "Smooth Rough Crinkly"

For this exercise you will need 3 bowls, and some assorted objects that fall into three categories:
1. Smooth Objects (River rocks, Polished stones, Felt, Velvet, Silk, Avocado Pit, etc.)
2. Rough Objects (Tree bark, Rope, Burlap, Squash, Avocado Skin, Corn Husk etc.)
3. Crinkly Objects (Wax Paper, Wrapping Paper, Autumn Leaves, Aluminum Foil etc.)

Keep the items small and manageable. Present the items one category at a time. As your baby explores each bowl say the name of the *object* they are handling clearly, and then say the corresponding *sensation*. Some parents choose to color code the three categories (i.e. Red = Smooth, Blue = Rough, Green = Crinkly) and then make or obtain 3 containers that correspond to the colors.

Caution: Depending on the size of some objects (i.e. river rocks) you will need to monitor closely to avoid a choking hazard.

Benefit: This activity helps your baby make cognitive associations between sensations and objects.

42. Helping Your Infant Eat Healthy

Adult's palates are influenced by what they were fed as babies. Anyone who doubts this may wonder why Australians are so fond of Vegemite (fermented Brewers Yeast) when no one else in the world can stomach it, and why Malaysians have a stomach for Durian, (a fruit considered so putrid that it's actually banned on airplanes) The reason Aussies eat Vegemite and Malaysians eat Durian is simple, they were raised eating it! The lesson is obvious: If you want your children to love nutrient rich foods, make a practice of introducing them to healthy foods early on. Start by compiling a list of fruits* and vegetables** on a white board or a blackboard. Include staples such as: apples, bananas, oranges, grapes, strawberries, blueberries, celery, papaya, mango, guava, pitted dates, figs, red bell pepper etc. Most babies enjoy bananas, grapes, or strawberries. Let us assume that your baby takes to grapes. In, a blender, blend 10 grapes with 1 celery stick. If your baby enjoys the drink, continue on this regimen for 2 weeks. Then gradually reduce the grapes (or increase the celery) and see if your baby still enjoys it. You may use this formula to introduce any new fruit or vegetable to an infants diet.

Benefit: Due to the high amount of sugars in most foods, many adolescents today do not enjoy consuming fruits and vegetables, simply because they were never introduced to them. Introducing your children to healthy foods early on will increase the odds that they will enjoy them for their rest of their lives.

*Some fruits, such as grapes can pose a choking hazard.
**I recommend organic fruits and vegetables

43. Activity: Make a Family Album

Make a chronological family album that shows individual pictures of each member of the family. Flip through the album on a regular basis and speak aloud the names of family members. When a family member visits, take baby over and show them their picture. Add new pictures to the album on a consistent day each month (i.e. the first Sunday, or the 12th day, etc.) New pictures should include baby, and any new editions to the family. Don't forget to include pictures of pets! **Benefit:** Teaching your baby about relatives honors their lineage. It also helps baby associate names with faces and\or voices. Most families I have worked with find this tradition very fun in the present, and very poignant when they reflect upon it.

44. Activity: Play board games with your spouse\partner

Traditional board games, such as Life, Sorry, Yatzee, Checkers, Parcheesi, Battleship, and Jenga, bond parents while providing a fascinating experience for babies. As board games can be played on the floor, babies feel included when they can help roll dice or move pieces. Long duration games (such as Monopoly and Risk) should be avoided. Instead choose simple, one-dimensional games such as the ones suggested above. All of which can be interrupted and restarted should baby need to nurse or eliminate. Always be careful to keep small pieces away from baby's mouth.

Benefit: As a new parent, you will likely be spending a lot of time at home. I find many parents actually become more distant after having a baby together. While one parent is tending to the babies needs, the other spends time reading, working, sleeping, and watching TV. Playing board games will allow you to have some free fun with your spouse and baby simultaneously.

45. Sign Language

Babies will feel a desire to communicate long before their lips and tongues are strong enough to do so. I find that many parents who are resistant to sign language fear that it may be too complex. The secret to baby signing is to teach 8 basic words, incorporating them one at a time:

1. Drink
2. More
3. Need to eliminate
4. Finished
5. Hungry
6. Toy
7. Mom
8. Dad

Benefit: Studies demonstrate that babies who learn basic sign language at about six months develop more cognitive passageways sooner, have higher I.Q's, and may have fewer tantrums. Maria Montessori believed that anything that empowers your baby to communicate their needs and feelings is a valuable resource.

46. Allow Your Child To Help You

When you are performing simple chores such as putting away laundry, stacking the dishwasher, or wiping counters, let your child assist you in the activity. What feels like work to you may prove fascinating to them. Start by asking for their help. When they join you, give them the simplest task possible, and then build on that foundation by teaching them each coinciding step. Maria Montessori's famous rule was: "Never help a child with a task at which he feels he can succeed."

Benefit: Doing chores early on prepares children for adolescent chores. This helps them feel valued and stimulated.

47. Be a Model to your Child

As your child matures, she will begin to take after you. If you speak impolitely to her, if you curse at people in traffic, if you argue in a petty manner with your spouse, she will absorb how you are behaving, and, if your bad behavior is consistent, she will begin to display the same attributes, albeit on a smaller scale. On the other hand, if you are patient, courteous, kind, tender, and loving, your child is more likely to display those qualities.

Benefit: If you devote yourself to being a better parent, your child will help you become one.

48. The Easiest Way to Teach Your Child a Second Language

During the first year of life, your baby is primed for learning that will carry them over for the rest of their lives. Due to the benefits of being multi-lingual, consider the two easiest methods for helping your child become multi-lingual child.

Option One: Enroll your child in a Montessori Friendly, *Foreign Language Immersion Daycare.*

Depending on where you live there may a day care which both satisfies the Montessori Guidelines, and which features immersion. Japanese, French, and Spanish are the most popular languages for immersion daycares.

Option Two: Hire a long term, multi-lingual nanny who will speak to your baby in their native tongue. Ask your nanny to refrain from English whenever possible. Studies show that if you can immerse your baby for the first three years, there is a stronger chance they will be proficient in both languages for the rest of their lives.

Benefits: The benefits of being multilingual are almost too many to name. Multilingual people have more career opportunities, more romance opportunities, and tend to earn more then the non-multilingual peers they grew up with.

49. An Alternative to the Word 'No'

In Montessori, we try to limit our use of the word No. Our goal isn't to stop children from bad things; it's to redirect them toward better things. Because we understand that our children are going to need some practice, we understand that we, as guardians, also deserve some practice (and some credit!). So before your baby becomes a toddler, practice saying the phrase: "Let's see if we can find a better way." Every day. When your child reaches six months, you should be a veritable master. Let's use an example. Let's say you are holding your baby at the dinner table. He shifts forward and reaches for a water glass, almost certain to knock it over. Instead of yelling out "NO!" Try to calmly redirect: "Let's see if we can a better way," In this example your baby might be wanting to grab something, so you might give him a toy to satiate his curiosity

Benefits: Redirecting helps ease tensions between parent and child. Avoiding 'No's' boosts self-esteem. When dealing with children, too many no's (by a parent) may be a sign that there is not enough of a foundation in the environment, or improper direction by the parent.

50. Invest in Swimming lessons

Although not directly addressed by Maria Montessori, I strongly believe that after a baby reaches six months, it is more often than not, a good idea to invest in swimming lessons with a reputable teacher. Swimming provides movement, expression, exercise, and a sense of freedom. Learning to swim is also recommended for safety. Even if you don't own a pool or live near a body of water, learning to swim early means that if you need to swim (to rescue someone, or due to a crisis such as a flood) you will be able to. Swimming is can also be important for socialization later in life.

Benefits: Swimming strengthens muscles, is a low impact exercise, and is fun.

51. Evaluate What's Working

The Montessori method is a framework for developing a healthy, autonomous, well-rounded child. Because every baby is unique it is recommended that you evaluate what is (and what is not) working with your individual baby every three months, and then adapt or modify any of the bullet points above. The Montessori System should not be taken as Gospel; it should be regarded as a method that is constantly evolving, just like babies are.

Benefit: Evaluating what's working, and modifying practices and environments accordingly will help ensure that your baby grows up to be as happy, healthy, strong, as they can be.